Donald k. Cilley

BARIATRIC SURGERY

Weight loss surgery guidelines

First edition

This book was professionally typeset on Reedsy
Find out more at reedsy.com

Contents

Will I lose weight if I convert to a vegetarian diet?

I'm attempting to get thinner. Protein smoothies might be useful.

Is phentermine a viable weight-loss option?

Can natural diuretics aid with weight loss and minimize fluid retention?

Introduction

a word used to describe surgical operations that alter the digestive tract to help in weight loss. Gastric bypass and other weight loss surgeries, as well as other procedures, can all be referred to as "bariatric surgery." Bariatric operations are all fairly serious treatments even though they all operate differently.

Bariatric surgery

$\mathbf{M}$aking Differences to your digestive tract is a element of bariatric surgery, which includes gastric bypass and other weight- loss procedures. When diet and exercise have failed or when you're passing major health issues as a result of your weight, bariatric surgery is performed. Your capability to eat further is confined by several procedures. Other treatments work by making it harder for the body to absorb nutrients. Some processes combine both.Even though there are multitudinous advantages to bariatric surgery, it's a substantial procedure with significant pitfalls and negative goods. To help assure the long- term success of bariatric surgery, you must also permanently acclimate your diet and engage in regularexercise.TypesBPD DS, or biliopancreatic diversion with duodenal switch stomach bypass(Roux- en-Y) Gastric sleeve surgery

Why is it done

Bariatric surgery is performed to help you in losing redundant weight and lower your threat of serious, perhaps fatal, weight- related health issues, similar asA heart attack and a stroke elevated blood pressureNonalcoholic steatohepatitis, frequently known as nonalcoholic adipose liver complaint(NAFLD)(NASH) Slumber apnea diabetes type 2 Generally speaking, bariatric surgery is only performed after you've made an trouble to reduce weight by altering your eating and exercise routines.

Who it's for In general,

you might be a seeker for bariatric surgery if You have a body mass indicator(BMI) of at least 40.(extreme rotundity). You have an rotundity- related serious health issues, similar as type 2 diabetes, high blood pressure, or severe sleep apnea, and your BMI is between 35 and39.9(rotundity). still, you might be eligible for some types of weight- loss surgery, If your BMI is between 30 and 34 and you have major weight- related health issues.Not everyone who's extremely fat should have bariatric surgery. To be eligible for weight- loss surgery, you might need to fulfill specific medical conditions. You will presumably go through a rigorous webbing process to discover if you qualify. To live a healthier life, you must also be prepared to make long- term adjustments.Long- term follow- up programs that track your diet, way of life, and geste

as well as your health issues may be anticipated of you.Additionally, bear in mind the cost of bariatric surgery. To find out if similar surgery is covered by your health insurance plan, communicate your original Medicare or Medicaid Office.Bariatric surgery has possible health hazards, both in the short and long term, just like any major procedure.The following are some implicit pitfalls of the surgical procedure a lot of blood Infection negative goods of anesthesiaClots of blood breathing or lung issues gastrointestinal system leaks Death(rare) Depending on the type of operation, different long- term pitfalls and consequences can affect from weight loss surgery. They may correspond of intestine blockageDumping pattern, which causes nausea, puking, flushing, dizziness, and diarrhea Gallstones Hernia reduced blood sugar(hypoglycemia) MalnutritionUlcersVomitingreflux of acidthe demand for a alternate or modification operation Death(rare)

How you get ready

Your medical platoon will give you with information on how to get ready for your particular type of surgery if you're a seeker for bariatric surgery. Before surgery, you might need to have a number of lab tests and examinations. There can be limitations on what you can eat, drink, and which medicines you can use. You might be forced to give up smoking and begin a physical exertionregimen.You might also need to get ready by organizing your post-surgery recovery in advance. Organize backing at home, for case, if you anticipate demanding it.What to anticipate General anesthesia is used for bariatric surgery to be performed in a sanitarium. This indicates that you were asleep throughout the process.Your unique circumstances, the type of weight- loss surgery you choose, and the sanitarium's or croaker

's programs will all have an impact on the specifics of your procedure. Some procedures to help you lose weight involve making long, open lacerations in your abdomen.

The maturity of bariatric procedures are now carried out

1aparoscopically. A laparoscope is a little camera- equipped tube- shaped device. Small abdominal lacerations are used to introduce the laparoscope. The surgeon can see within your tummy and do procedures there without using the conventionally huge lacerations thanks to the bitsy camera on the laparoscope's tip. Although laparoscopic surgery can dock and speed up your rehabilitation, not everyone is a goodcandidate.The average surgery lasts several hours. You awaken in a recovery room following surgery, where medical labor force keeps an eye out for any issues. You might have to spend a couple of days in the sanitarium, depending on your surgery.Bariatric surgery types Each type of bariatric surgery has advantages and disadvantages. Make sure to bandy them with your croaker

. There are some exemplifications of typical bariatric surgery procedures Roux- en- Y gastric bypass(roo- en- wy). The most popular fashion for gastric bypass is this process. generally, this procedure can not be reversed. It functions by limiting the quantum of food you can eat at one time and lowering nutrition absorption.Your stomach's top is separated from the rest of it by a cut made by the surgeon. Only roughly an ounce of food may fit in the performing poke

, which is roughly the size of a walnut. Your stomach can generally store three pints offood.The small intestine is also incompletely sliced and darned onto the poke

by the surgeon. Food also enters this little stomach poke

and travels right to the small intestine that's attached to it. Food enters your small intestine directly into the middle half, skipping much of your stomach and the first part of theintestine.gastric sleeve surgery. By removing around 80 of the stomach during a sleeve gastrectomy, a long, tube- suchlike poke

is left before. There's lower room for food in this lower stomach. also, it generates lower ghrelin, a hormone that controls appetite, which may reduce your appetite toeat.This treatment has benefits including considerable weight loss and no gut rerouting. also, compared to utmost other procedures, a sleeve gastrectomy requires a shorter sanitariumstay.Duodenal switch with biliopancreatic diversion. In the first stage of this two- part treatment, a sleeve gastrectomy- suchlike fashion is carried out. Bypassing the maturity of the intestine, the alternate procedure(duodenal switch and biliopancreatic diversion) connects the terminal portion of the intestine to the duodenum close to thestomach.This procedure both restricts how important you can consume and decreases nutrient immersion. Although it's relatively successful, there are advanced pitfalls associated with it, similar as starvation and vitamindeficiencies.The ideal weight- loss surgery for you'll depend on your unique circumstances. Body mass indicator, eating habits, other health conditions, former surgeries, and the troubles associated with each procedure are just a many of the variables that your surgeon will consider.after weight loss surgery You will not frequently be permitted to eat for one to two days following weight- loss surgery so that your stomach and digestive system can heal. After that, you will cleave to a particular diet for many weeks. The diet starts out with only liquids, proceeds to pureed, extremely soft foods, and eventually includes ordinary foods. How important and what you can eat and drink may be subject to a variety of limitations orrestrictions.In the original months following weight- loss surgery, you'll also suffer routine medical examinations to track your health. You might bear multitudinous checks, blood work, and laboratory tests.

Results

Long- lasting weight loss can be achieved by gastric bypass and other bariatric procedures. The type of surgery you suffer and the variations you make to your life will affect how important weight you lose. Within two times, you might be suitable to reduce half or maybe further of your redundantweight.In addition to helping cases lose weight, gastric bypass surgery has been shown to ameliorate or treat a number of diseases linked to rotundity, similar asHeart condition elevated blood pressure Obstructive snoring diabetes type 2 Nonalcoholic steatohepatitis, frequently known as nonalcoholic adipose liver complaint(NAFLD)(NASH) The complaint of gastroesophageal influx(GERD) Osteoarthritis(common pain) also, gastric bypass surgery might increase your capacity for common everyday tasks, which may enhance your quality of life.When weight loss surgery is unsuccessfulOther weight- loss procedures like gastric bypass do not always work as well as you might have allowed

. You might not lose weight and experience major health issues if a weight- loss surgery does not work or stops working.After having weight- loss surgery, keep all of your listed follow- up movables

Consult your croaker

right down if you realize that you aren't losing weight or if you witness problems. You can track your weight reduction and assess any variables that might be holding you back from losing weight.Even if the process itself is successful, it's still possible for the case to fail to lose enough weight or to gain it back after having any kind of weight- loss surgery.However, similar as adding your physical exertion and eating healthier refections, weight gain may affect, If you don't make the suggested life adjustments.weight- loss vitamin patchesIt's critical to continue taking your diurnal vitamins and minerals after bariatric surgery. This is because you may not be suitable to absorb nutrients as well as you formerly did because your digestive system isn't what it was previous to surgery.However, being instructed to take a supplement every day may be intimidating, If you dislike taking medications.You may have therefore heard of a bariatric vitamin patch, which you apply to your skin and also forget about till the end of the day.However, it presumably is, as the saying goes, If commodity seems too good to be true. One of those cases is this one. Learn further about bariatric vitamin patches below, including how they serve and why they might not be sufficient for those who have experienced bariatric surgery.Gastric bypass surgery demand individualities who suffer weight loss surgery should be taking some form of the bariatric vitamin exploration indicates that all bariatric surgery cases are at threat for scarcities in folate, vitamins B1, B12, A, C, K, and D, as well as iron, zinc, selenium, andcopper.

Weight- loss surgery changes the shape and function of your digestive system.

This surgery may help you lose weight and manage medical conditions related to rotundity. These conditions include diabetes, obstructive sleep apnea, and threat factors for heart complaint and stroke.the most common weight- loss surgery is the sleeve gastrectomy. In this procedure, the surgeon removes a large portion of the stomach to produce a tubelike sleeve.Weight- loss surgery is only one part of an overall treatment plan. Your treatment will also include nutrition guidelines, exercise, and internal health care. You will need to be willing and suitable to follow this long- term plan to achieve your weight- loss goals.However, you will meet with a number of specialists to help you decide if weight- loss surgery is an option for you, If you are considering weight- losssurgery.Medical guidelinesThe general medical guidelines for weight- loss surgery are grounded on body mass indicator(BMI). BMI is a formula that uses weight and height to estimate body fat. Weight- loss surgery might be an option for an adult with a BMI of 40 or higher.The surgery may also be an option for an grown-up who meets these three conditions BMI of 35 or higherAt least one rotundity- related medical condition At least six months of supervised weight- loss attemptsIn some cases, weight- loss surgery may be an option for adolescents. The guidelines includeBMI of 40 or advanced and any rotundity- related medical condition BMI of 35 or advanced and a severe rotundity- related medical condition Instead of using these BMI figures as a guideline for surgery, a surgeon may use growth maps for adolescents. These maps show the standard BMI range for each age. The surgeon may recommend the procedure grounded on how much the adolescent's BMI is above the standard BMI range.Depending on the type or inflexibility of an rotundity- related illness, some grown-ups or adolescents with lower BMIs may be suitable to suffer weight- loss surgery.

How to know if you are ready for surgery

If you are considering weight- loss surgery, you will meet with a health care platoon that may include the following Primary care doctor Surgeon Anesthesiologist DietitianA nanny specializing in weight management Psychologist or psychiatristOther specialists depending on your medical conditions Members of your platoon will explain what to anticipate ahead and after the procedure. They will estimate whether you are ready for surgery and help you decide if it's an option for you. They may identify enterprises to address — medical, behavioral, or cerebral — ahead you are ready for surgery.Medical concerns You will have a medical test to diagnose any unknown rotundity- related conditions.

Your croaker

also will test for problems that could make surgery more complicated. You may suffer tests for Sleep apnea Cardiovascular disease,Kidney disease, Liver disease You will probably not be suitable to have surgery if you have these conditions Blood- clotting disorders Severe heart complaint that prohibits the safe use of anesthesia Other conditions that increase the threat of using anesthesia Behaviors and internal health Weight loss after surgery depends on your capability to change actions in eating and exercise. Also, being in good internal health is important for the demands of following your treatment plan. Your platoon's pretensions are to identify cerebral or behavioral threat factors, address any problems, and decide whether you are ready for surgery.

Your health care platoon will talk with you about the followingMotivation. Are you motivated to embrace life changes, set pretensions, and educate yourself about healthy nutrition? Your platoon will track your capability to follow recommended changes to your diet and exercise routine.Weight- loss history.

What overeating and exercise plans have you used in the history to lose weight?

Did you lose weight or recapture weight?

Patterns in weight loss and weight gain can help your platoon understand challenges for you and recommend strategies for post-surgical plans.Eating actions. Irregular eating actions or eating diseases may contribute to rotundity. These include binge eating, darkness eating, and unplanned grazing between refections. Some eating diseases are associated with other mood diseases and other internal health conditions.Mood diseases. Depression, anxiety, bipolar complaint, or other mood diseases are associated with rotundity, and these conditions may make it delicate to manage your weight. Also, people with undressed mood diseases frequently find it delicate to stick with new diet and exercise habits after surgery.Alcohol and medicine use. Problems with alcohol or medicine use, as well as smoking, are associated with poor weight loss and continued substance use problems after surgery. undressed or unmanaged problems likely enjoin the option of weight-losssurgery.Suicide threat. There's an increased threat of self-murder among people who have experienced weight-loss surgery. The threat is advanced among people with depression, anxiety, bipolar complaint, substance use complaint, schizophrenia, or other disorders.

Pre- surgery expectations

I f your platoon members recommend bariatric surgery, they will work with you to develop a treatment plan. This may include Nutrition guidelines. The dietitian will help you with nutrition guidelines, vitamin supplements, and menu planning. The guidelines include changes ahead and aftersurgery.Exercise plan. A nanny , occupational therapist, or other specialists will help you learn applicable exercises, develop an exercise plan, and set goals.Weight loss. You may be encouraged or needed to lose some weight through diet and exercise before you can have surgery.Psychotherapy. You may be needed to begin talk remedy, medicine treatment, or other internal health remedy to treat an eating complaint, depression, or other internal health condition. Your remedy may include developing new managing chops or addressing your enterprises about body image or tone-esteem.Smoking.However, you will be asked to quit smoking or share in a program to help you quit, If you smoke.

Other treatments.

You will be anticipated to follow treatments for other medical conditions.These conditions are intended to help you achieve the stylish possible weight- loss issues after surgery. Also, your capability to follow through on these plans will show your platoon how motivated you're to follow guidelines after surgery. Weight- loss surgery can be delayed or canceled if your health care platoon determines thatYou are not psychologically or medically ready for surgery You have not made applicable changes in your eating or exercise habits You gained weight during the evaluation process

Paying for surgery

Your insurance company may cover the costs of weight- loss surgery. Your platoon will need to show that the procedure is medically necessary. Also, you may need to give proved substantiation that you were not suitable to lose enough weight with a supervised program of diet and exercise. Medicare and some Medicaid programs may cover thecosts.It's important to probe your insurance content and your anticipated out- of- fund costs. Your sanitarium may have services to help you explore options for financing your surgery.

Is bariatric surgery right for you?

A** platoon of croakers**, nursers, and other specialists will help you determine whether this is an applicable option for you.The process the platoon uses to determine if you are ready for weight- loss surgery is also there to help you make an informed decision. You'll need to consider the benefits and pitfalls, follow through with pre-surgery and post-surgery plans, and make a lifelong commitment to a new nutrition and exercise program.

What's gastric bypass weight- loss surgery?

Roux- en- Y gastric bypass(RYGB) is a type of weight-loss surgery. Weight- loss surgery is also called bariatric surgery. It's frequently done as a laparoscopic surgery, with small lacerations in the abdomen.This surgery reduces the size of your upper stomach to a small poke

about the size of an egg. The surgeon does this by stapling off the upper section of the stomach. This reduces the quantum of food you can eat. The surgeon also attaches this poke

directly to a part of the small intestine called the Roux branch. This forms a" Y" shape. The food you eat also bypasses the rest of the stomach and the upper part of your small intestine. This reduces the quantum of fat and calories you absorb from the foods you eat. It also reduces the number of vitamins and minerals you absorb from food.

Why would I bear gastric bypass surgery for weightloss?

Significant rotundity is treated with gastric bypass surgery. For those who have tried indispensable weight loss ways without long- term success, it's encouraged.However, your croaker

might recommend gastric bypass surgery, If you have a body mass indicator(BMI) of 40 or over and are extremely obese.However, high blood pressure, heart complaint, If you have a BMI of 35 to 40 and a medical issue like sleep apnea.About 100 pounds of redundant weight can be lost with the aid of a gastric bypass. also, it might reverse type 2 diabetes and exclude influx and heartburn. also, having weight- loss surgery can reduce your threat of developing cardiac issues, sleep apnea, and high blood pressure.

What are the troubles of having a gastric bypass procedure?

Any surgery could affect in side goods including bleeding, infection, and blood clots in your legs. also, respiratory issues or other responses could affect from general anesthesia. also, the Roux branch or stomach poke may be leaking.Long- term issues that could arise include If you do not take supplements every day for the rest of your life, you will have low quantities of vitamins.low calcium and iron levels difficulty consuming enough protein Syndrome of the dump. This may affect in diarrhea after eating, dizziness, nausea, and rapid-fire heartbeat.a narrowing of the bowel' joining points(stenosis or stricture) An internal hernia that can be fatal since the small intestine can come entrapped and plugged Additional surgery is required unable to reduce weight sufficiently If you nibble on high- calorie foods and do not exercise, you may acquire weight.Depending on your health, you can face fresh hazards. Prior to the procedure, make sure to bandy any worries you may have with your healthcare staff.

How should I prepare for a Roux-en-Y gastric bypass?

Gastric bypass surgery must first be approved by your medical team as a viable choice for you. For those who misuse drugs or alcohol, or who can't commit to a long-term change in lifestyle, weight-loss surgery is not recommended.

You must engage in a bariatric surgery education program before undergoing surgery. You can use this to get ready for surgery and for life afterward. You'll receive nutritional guidance. Additionally, you might undergo psychiatric testing. You'll also require tests and physical examinations. Blood testing is required. upper endoscopy or imaging tests of your stomach are both options.

Smokers must give up several months prior to surgery. Before surgery, your surgeon can advise you to reduce your weight. Your liver will become smaller, as a result, making surgery safer. In the days leading up to your surgery, you must cease taking aspirin, ibuprofen, and other blood-thinning medications. Prior to surgery, you shouldn't consume any food or liquids after midnight.

What takes place throughout a Roux-en-Y gastric bypass procedure?

Typically, the procedure takes several hours.

For your surgery, general anesthesia will be used. As a result, you won't feel any pain during the procedure and will sleep through it.

Laparoscopy may be used by your surgeon. Your abdomen will receive a number of tiny cuts (incisions) from him or her. The surgeon will next use these incisions to introduce a laparoscope and small surgical instruments.

The upper portion of your stomach will be cut into a small pouch by the surgeon using a laparoscopic stapler.

The upper portion of your small intestine is then divided into a tube with two ends using the stapler.

The Roux limb, which is the small intestine's upper end, is taken up to the stomach pouch where a little link, or anastomosis, is formed. The small intestine's other end is then joined to another section of the small intestine.

Then, your surgeon might perform an upper endoscopy or a dye study to check for leakage.

What happens following a Roux-en-Y gastric bypass?

After the surgery, you can spend one or two days in the hospital. Discuss with your doctor how to treat wounds, use safe painkillers, and when to begin exercising. How frequently to change the dressing over your wound will be specified by your doctor.

If you experience any of the following, call your physician straight away:

Fever

Your wound starts to hurt, feels hot to the touch, or starts to leak fluid.

coughing or breathing issues

diarrhea and gagging

Legs, shoulders, chest, or stomach pain

Any further issues or signs

For the first one to two weeks following surgery, you will probably only be able to consume liquids. Around a month after surgery, your doctor may have you gradually introduce soft food and eventually conventional meals to your diet. You must chew thoroughly and slowly, and you must wait 30 minutes between drinking and eating.

It's critical to acquire all the nutrition and vitamins you require as you recuperate because the first weight loss you experience may happen quickly. For vitamins and minerals that your body might no longer be able to adequately absorb from food alone, your doctor will prescribe supplements.

Following gastric bypass surgery, many doctors advise the following:

multivitamins are taken daily. You ought to take a daily multivitamin with 200% of the recommended daily amounts.

daily supplements with calcium. Calcium-containing multivitamins might not safeguard bone health. Each day, you might require 1,600–2,000 IU of vitamin D and 1,600 mg of calcium. After taking your multivitamin, take a calcium supplement at least two hours later.

B-12 vitamin supplements

All patients who have undergone weight loss surgery are advised to take vitamin B-12 supplements to help avoid bone fractures. Several times a week, you can take this by mouth. You could also receive monthly B-12 injections.

oral supplements with vitamin D. If your levels are low, you could require this. Your doctor might advise taking 50,000 IU of vitamin D2 orally once a week for eight weeks. Some people need vitamin D supplements their entire lives.

supplements with iron The amount of iron in a multivitamin may not be sufficient to avoid anemia after gastric bypass surgery. You could require an extra 50–100 mg of elemental iron each day. Vitamin C will aid in the body's absorption of iron. Find out from your doctor what dosage is ideal for you.

Experts advise having your blood checked at least every six months for the rest of your life to make sure you are getting the proper quantity of vitamins and minerals because nutritional deficits can occur following this procedure.

You can have temporary hair thinning, dry skin, mood swings, bodily aches, and fatigue while losing weight. These issues ought to disappear once your weight stabilizes. A year or so into the process, weight loss will halt. If the pouch stretches after a year, you might be able to eat more. The first year should be used to establish healthy diet and exercise routines that will prevent you from gaining weight again.

You will probably see a dietician in addition to your doctor's and surgeon's follow-up sessions, who will instruct you on how and what to consume given your smaller stomach. If your lifestyle has changed, you might also need to consult a psychologist to help you deal with your feelings and worries.

Next actions

Be sure to understand the following before consenting to the test or procedure:

The test or procedure's name

The purpose of the test or operation you are undergoing

What outcomes to anticipate, and what they signify

The test's or procedure's advantages and disadvantages

What the potential negative consequences or difficulties might be

When and where the test or operation will be performed

Who will conduct the test or procedure and what credentials they possess

What would occur if the test or procedure weren't performed?

Any alternatives to consider in terms of testing or processes When and how will you receive the results

Who to contact if you have concerns or issues following the test or process

How much will the examination or procedure cost?

Are injections of vitamin B-12 effective for shedding pounds?

There is no conclusive proof that injections of vitamin B-12 promote weight loss.

Meat, fish, and dairy products are just a few examples of foods that naturally contain the water-soluble vitamin B-12, which belongs to the B complex. Additionally, certain foods have vitamin B-12 added to them, and it is also sold as a nutritional supplement. Injections of vitamin B-12 are frequently used to treat or prevent B-12 deficiency and pernicious anemia.

Injections of vitamin B-12 are provided by several weight-loss clinics as a component of their weight-loss regimens. The benefits of vitamin B-12 injections, according to proponents, include increased energy and a boosted metabolism that aid in weight loss. However, vitamin B-12 injections are unlikely to provide you with more energy unless you are vitamin B-12 deficient.

Metformin (Fortamet, Glucophage, Riomet) is a medication that is occasionally used by persons with type 2 diabetes as part of a weight-loss plan. An adverse effect of this medication may be a lack of vitamin B-12. If you use metformin, talk to your doctor about ways to keep your B-12 levels in a healthy range.

It's unlikely that receiving high doses of vitamin B-12 via injections will be harmful to your health. But if you get vitamin B-12 injections, be sure to let your doctor know because it can affect how well some medications work.

Avoid being seduced by quick fixes if you want to reduce weight. A healthy lifestyle is what really matters. Enjoy healthier foods in moderation and make exercise a part of your daily routine.

Will I lose weight if I convert to a vegetarian diet?

No, not always. Being vegetarian is more of a lifestyle choice than it is a diet that promotes weight loss.

However, it is true that vegetarians tend to be typically slimmer than non-vegetarians, both as adults and as children. This might be the case because a vegetarian diet often places a greater emphasis on fruits, vegetables, nutritious grains, and plant-based proteins—foods that are more satisfying, and lower in calories, and fat.

However, a vegetarian diet is not always minimal in calories. On a vegetarian diet, you can gain weight if you consume excessive amounts of high-calorie foods such as sweetened beverages, fried foods, snacks, and sweets.

Even some vegetarian meals, such as soy hot dogs, soy cheese, refried beans, and snack bars, can be rich in calories and fat.

Whether you stay away from animal products or not, eating a nutritious diet and balancing your caloric intake with your caloric expenditure are the keys to reaching and maintaining a healthy weight.

I'm attempting to get thinner. Protein smoothies might be useful.

P rotein shake producers may claim that their goods aid in weight loss or reduce body fat. However, protein shakes aren't a secret weapon for weight loss.

According to several findings, increasing your daily protein intake may have advantages. For instance, consuming foods or beverages high in protein may help you reduce body fat, maintain lean muscle, feel satisfied, and lose weight. But the proof is scant. Additionally, studies examine a variety of protein sources, not only protein shakes.

You may be able to lose weight by reducing your daily calorie intake by substituting protein shakes for meals. But eventually, you'll have to resume eating solid food. If you don't make wise dietary decisions, eating solid food could make your excess weight come back. Additionally, you'll miss out on the health advantages of entire foods if you overly rely on protein drinks to take the place of your daily meals.

Protein contains calories, therefore eating too much of it may make it more difficult to lose weight. This may occur if you consume protein drinks in addition to your regular diet without cutting back on calories or exercising.

According to the Dietary Guidelines for Americans, the daily requirement for protein for an average adult is between 46 and 56 grams. This sum is based on your weight and general state of health. You probably don't need to add extra protein from protein shakes or other sources as long as you maintain a nutritious diet.

Keep in mind that burning more calories than you consume is the key to reducing weight. Select nutritious foods, such as:

Fruits\sVegetables

Brown rice or whole-wheat bread are examples of entire grains.

dairy items with low or no fat content, such as milk, yogurt, and cheese

Skinless chicken breasts, eggs, seafood, beans, peas, lentils, soy products, almonds, and seeds are examples of foods high in protein.

Additionally, try to limit your intake of foods with extra salt, sugar, or saturated fat.

Include exercise in your regular routine as well. On most days of the week, aim for 30 minutes of exercise, such as brisk walking. Additionally, strengthen all main muscle groups at least twice per week.

Is phentermine a viable weight-loss option?

An amphetamine-like prescription drug called phentermine (Adipex-P, Lomaira) is used to decrease appetite. reducing your appetite or prolonging your feeling of fullness, can aid in weight loss. For weight loss, phentermine and topiramate are also offered (Qsymia).

Phentermine is meant to be taken as part of a comprehensive weight-loss program, just like other prescription weight-loss medications. It is not recommended for those who only wish to lose a few pounds; rather, it is for those who are obese and have tried unsuccessfully to reduce enough weight with food and exercise alone.

The classification of Schedule IV medicines, which includes phentermine, designates substances with a low likelihood of abuse but a possibility for abuse nonetheless.

The following are phentermine's typical adverse effects:

-higher heart rate
  -Prickles or tingles in the hands or feet
  -mouth ache
  -Sleeplessness
  -Nervousness
  -Constipation

Although one of the most frequently recommended weight-loss drugs is phentermine, those with heart disease, high blood pressure, an overactive thyroid gland, or glaucoma shouldn't consider this prescription. Additionally, it's not appropriate for women who are or might be pregnant or who are nursing.

Can natural diuretics aid with weight loss and minimize fluid retention?

You may be able to eliminate water with the help of several herbs and dietary supplements, which can also help with sodium and water retention. Dandelion, ginger, parsley, hawthorn, and juniper are a few examples. Before using any products that have a diuretic effect, however, act with caution.

Numerous medical disorders and some drugs can lead to fluid retention. Therefore, it's crucial to discuss potential causes of fluid retention with your doctor before attempting to cure it on your own. Additionally, some plants and supplements can exacerbate existing medical conditions or interact negatively with prescription drugs.

Theoretically, natural diuretics may reduce fluid retention by increasing urination. However, there is little to no scientific evidence to support the diuretic properties of these plants or supplements, so you might not find them to be useful.

Focus on eating a healthy diet, reducing your salt intake, and engaging in lots of physical activity — rather than taking diuretics — if you want to reduce water weight as part of your weight-loss objective or you're worried about water retention due to menstruation.

Never take nutritional supplements or herbal remedies without first consulting your doctor.